Shards
Of the
Urn

[Special Dedication Edition]

Poems by
Timothy Brannan

Cover Art: Original Painting by Timothy Brannan

Other works by
Timothy Brannan

'74: A Basketball Story
TEARS OF ALLAH
TEACH
THE END
Manhattan Spiritual
Into the Elephant Grass
Adventures in Another Paradise

© Timothy Brannan 2014
ISBN 978-0-9820277-6-9
Published in the United States of America
June 16, 2014
By Gemini Publishing LLC 2014

DEDICATED
To
Bob Hopkins

You lived life well, with vigor and virtue, and you are missed.

Robert Patton Hopkins was born June 16, 1943 one day before me. He was a son and brother. He was a husband and father. He was an engineer, a builder of useful and beautiful things. And, he was my friend for more than fifty years. Bob died May 25, 2009. I was working on some of these poems at the time. So, now that I have, at long last, completed this small volume of verse, I thought it would be appropriate to honor him by dedicating it to him and to his memory.

Ode to Bob

Everybody dies sometime
In the middle of a mountain climb
While thinking up another rhyme
Everybody dies

Why not me, then, we ask
When others pass
Before us.
Why not me?
How can this be?

Whatever plan there is
Exists beyond our knowing.
Whatever understanding there may be
Comes only with proper showing.
So, driving along I-95
To attend the funeral
Of a friend of mine,
I know this is
The way the world ends,
T.S., not with a bang,
Not with a whimper,
But with a nine-hour drive
Because you're the friend
Still left alive.

CONTENTS

DEDICATION: Ode to Bob

Shards of the Urn

It breaks my heart to view
what the world has done
to itself and to you.
The pieces it has left behind
are far too fragile and too few.

What shards of greatness
and of beauty
have we salvaged
from the urn?
What tales of loch ness
and of duty
have we scavenged
from the burn?

What oil and light show
still penetrates
so deep into
our souls?
What makes the eye glow
until it aches
as our story
still unfolds
in fragments of both your heart and mine
that lay spread upon a table?

Like innards, they draw the future's design,
a tale in the language of Babel
of the cruel necessity of the lance
in order to acquire
the hope that gives peace a chance
beyond survival and desire.

The naked shoals of oil and light

As the excrement hits the fan
As the foot kicks the can
As the wheat yields the bran
As the censor sets the ban,
muddled and befuddled we cross the blurry line
into a place where there is no sign
of what is yours or what is mine.
In that land, although mistakes abound
and creep about the knolls
where oil and light can still be found,
no one wrecks on the naked shoals
of being bundled in the bed
and sharing the same night coals
with the abiding symbol of the dead.

Schrödinger's Cat

A cat which is neither alive nor dead
leaves a lot that remains unsaid and said
for those who continue to zombie through life
never observing atoms of their own strife
because, to an inexplicable degree,
they don't take the time to see
inside the box that holds the cat
that tells us where all the atoms are at.

The *carpe diem* song

Carpe diem quam minimum credula postero.
Horace, *Odes*

Lost in time and space that is torn
we kill ourselves by being born,
but we only have to look behind
to see where we have traveled time
as one by one philosophies are embraced.

One by one embraces are erased.

One by one lives decline
As those who live them die.
One by one your life or mine
dissolves into a sigh.

Now that only photons remain
of what was once our stardust domain,
the great black hole we still call night
waits patiently for our final flight.

Eskimos have at least 100 words for snow

There must be
at least as many
words for love as
there are for snow.

There must be
at least as much
we delight in from joy as
we ache from sorrow.

Yet the heat of passion
melts the reason of
all we will ever know
as snow still covers tomorrow.

My Mother's Recipes

She hurled her recipes at life
like rolling pins
in a juggler's rage.
You had to learn agility
quickly
in a four-dimensional
kind of way
in order to survive.
Yet, at the end,
festered by age,
"Oh Gosh" was all she could muster
as the morphine blanket
ushered her
onto another stage.

I knew lust and I knew longing

[A Poem for Our 35th Wedding Anniversary]

I knew lust and
I knew longing.
I had a need for place
and belonging.

But,

I had killed and
I had plundered
thought and action.
Everywhere I'd blundered.

So,

what could I feel?
What could I think
peering over the edge
and into the brink?

Well,

I could feel nothing
and think even less,
living, as I was,
in persistent distress.

And,

I still didn't get it.
I didn't have a clue
until the first time
I encountered you.

Then,

my one hand clapped.
The way unnamed but clear
lay beneath me
transubstantiated from fear.

Still,

I couldn't keep away the dreams
that I slept beside
carcasses and
dying men's screams.

Yes,

I knew lust and
I knew longing.
I had a need for place
and a sense of belonging.

Yes,

I had killed and
I had plundered
thought and action.
Everywhere I'd blundered.

But,

I knew deep down
there was only one place true--
the land of the brave
And living with you.

Memorial Day 2007

Wrap me up
In that flag I earned
Back in sixty-eight.

Wrap me up
In that flag we know
As my last loved one sighs.

Wrap me up
In that flag of mine
When I go through the pearly gate.

Wrap me up
In those stripes and stars
The one for freedom flies.

Tethered by the contents

Tethered by the refuse of his memories,
trapped by the ruptures of his heart,
hope was a present from his enemies--
their ultimate weapon of last resort.
Wrapped in their half-truth sighs
offered in desperation to impart
the promise of liberation,
it blew apart
before his baffled eyes.

There Is a Reason We Die When We Do

There is a reason we
die when we do
if only I could
figure it out.

Somewhere amidst
the flotsam and
jetsam of time,
embracing the hopes
and dreams that cling
to the next rhyme,
it floats about--
searching for
what to accept
and what to doubt.

No cuttlefish or hybrid rose.
Only someone
other than me possibly knows.
But, perhaps, at least,
I can determine or decide
which word should be beast
and which should be bride.

The Essential Human Conflict

To leave no foot print along the path
or to leave a foot print that may last.
He had no idea which was switch
and which was lollipop
as he prepared for his next folly stop.

Was it yet another false choice,
or was it just poorly voiced?
Perhaps it was accurate beyond belief
and to be highly praised
because of the benign conundrum it raised.

After all, he had seen what foot prints make.
He'd been there at the beginning
with hearts of stone that would never break;
but he could not be around for the ending
when, even that, he felt sure they would forsake.

Into the winds of time

Into the winds of time we dive
riding the surf of currents that surge
inevitably toward shores of destiny
simply to remain alive.

With the opening of a hand,
The chute is loosed.
With the closing of a fist,
the ripcord is grasped.
All else I cannot understand
from the time wind sea and sand
until the answer is finally reduced.

Put everything through the filter.
Pitch your question into the grid.
But, never doubt the final answer
As you navigate the eternal skid.

The question is trick and slight-of-hand
So let's make the answer clear.
To procreate upon demand,
my love, is the reason we are here.

.

We Know Not What We Do

God forgive us for we know not what we do
when we let freedom evaporate
like springtime dew.
We used to stand for something more
than being the world's whore.
But now we turn the willing trick
and beat feet for the door.
It used to be we believed in the same
for all no matter what the name
no matter the fame
no matter the blame.
But now we turn the trick
and beg for more.
Then we beat feet for the open door.

The Theory of Everything

There is this idea out there somewhere
that everything can be explained,
that the scientist is most prescient
in predicting when it recently rained.

Well, I am here to remind all of us
that we have lost our collective minds.
There is no explanation to discuss.
It is simply the big bang that binds
us together in whatever hive we choose
no matter what we think of it,
no matter how much we lose.

The belief is merely a motet that sings
of all that is destined to come.
From black holes to vibrating membranes and strings,
it serenades us from the beyond.

If there is to ever be any change
from that established lore,
we will, likely, find it aimlessly arranged
under the easy chair or scattered across the floor
where the clotting dust of astral dissent
seems to have been heaven sent
as we sweep it out the door.

Brooding in the night gale

Fled is that music: Do I wake or sleep?
Ode to a Nightingale, **John Keats**

Brooding in the night gale,
The nightingale sang
Singing in the right scale
Her warble railed and rang
Of frustration and surrender
And inevitable sturm und drang
Brooding in the night gale
The nightingale sang

Could she ever sing again
With a meaning that was true
The songs that could mend
And make her happy too
Or would she continue
In her decrescendo
As her wings ruffled into
Winds of deceit and innuendo

Oh, brooding in the night gale
The nightingale sang
Singing in the right scale
Her warble railed and rang
Of frustration and surrender
And inevitable sturm und drang
Brooding in the night gale
The nightingale sang

What was that in the blow
Some verse she did not know
Some secret dance within the show

Oh no! Oh no!

It was the wail of her
Brooding in the night gale
Trying hard to tell her tale
Trying hard to set sail
On a course that
Will not be charted

Brooding in the night gale
The nightingale sang
Singing in the right scale
Her warble railed and rang
Of frustration and surrender
And inevitable sturm und drang
Brooding in the night gale
The nightingale sang

What was that in the blow
Some verse she did not know
Some secret dance within the show

Oh no! Oh no! Oh no!

It was the wail

Of her brooding in the right scale
It was the wail
Of her brooding in the night gale
Brooding in the night gale
The nightingale sang

Sitting on the edge of the earth

It seems like forever
Since I've tasted the wine
And the stale white wafers
On which we used to dine
I don't know that it matters—
Separation from the divine—
Since I've lived my life
Putting everything on the line
But this is my fate for living long
It is the cost of every song
To weep for the old ones
From before
And the young ones
Still to come
Yet, here I sit on the edge of the earth
No longer able to propagate the birth
Of songs and stories
Of regretted youth
In vain searches for unrealized truth

Once you've taken a step along
It's hard to un-step that way you're on
So consider the path you step upon
Or you may become some surveyor's pawn
Pounded into the edge of the world
Bound by no chain or flag unfurled

Only by that final refrain
And the feeling of that last drop of rain
Oh, this is my fate for living long
It is the cost of every song
To weep for the lovers that we have no more
And for the battles we never won
Yet, here I sit on the edge of the earth
No longer able to propagate the birth
Of the songs and the stories of regretted youth
In vain searches for unrealized truth

So, be careful what you learn
For you can never forget
Be careful what you yearn for
Or you could soon regret
Be careful what you hate
For you may quickly become it
But most of all
Be careful what you fear
For it may be the summit

Ah, this is my fate for living long
It is the cost of every song
To weep for the old ones from before
And the young ones still to come
To weep for the lovers we have no more
And the wars we never won
Yet, here I sit on the edge of the earth
No longer able to propagate the birth

Of the songs and the stories of regretted youth
In vain searches for that unrealized truth
This is my fate for living long
It is the cost of every song . . . .

About the Author

Timothy Brannan is a novelist, poet, composer, and painter, born and raised in Raleigh, North Carolina. He holds a Bachelor of Arts in English and Philosophy and a Master of Arts in Literature and Writing from North Carolina State University. Both as an undergraduate and a graduate student he was mentored by the late Dr. Guy Owen (*Ballad of the Flim-Flam Man, Journey for Joedel, The White Stallion and Other Poems*). With Guy's help, he submitted the first pioneering creative writing Master's thesis ever accepted at North Carolina State University nearly thirty years before the university established an official writing program. Timothy later earned an Ed.S. from Appalachian State University and a Juris Doctor from Florida State University.

After serving in Vietnam in Army Military Intelligence and Psychological Operations, he returned to the USA and traveled around the country and Mexico. He met his life soul mate, Lana Zimmerman, while working for a major publisher in New York. They left the city and traveled the country in a yellow International Travel-All—their own version of the Merry Pranksters bus. After marrying in 1972, they pursued Masters Degrees at NC State University. Upon graduation, they followed Lana's job offer to the mountains of North Carolina where Timothy eventually taught GED in a youthful offender prison. In 1978 they moved to St. Thomas, USVI where Timothy first taught drama at a day camp on Megan's Bay Beach and later served as one of the creators and the Chief of Staff for the USVI Senate Democratic Caucus. In that capacity, he was instrumental in the Virgin Islands being included in President Ronald Reagan's initial Caribbean Basin Initiative and in developing legislation that essentially rescued the Virgin Islands economy. Until his retirement to write full time, Timothy served as chief of staff, legal counsel, and political consultant for a wide range of government entities, elected officials, political campaigns and interest groups.